WROXHAM

The Capital of the Broads

WROXHAM AND HOVETON

There is Wroxham, set upon the River Bure, seven miles from Norwich, an admirable collection of thatched cottages, tall hedges, rose-gardens, rustics and clucking hens... Wroxham had cast its spell on us.

Thus wrote an American visitor in 1895, in an article published in *The Century Magazine* in November of that year. She went on to describe in detail her conversation with John Loynes, probably the first to recognise the potential for hire craft on the Broads, and a key figure in the growth of Wroxham.

Less than 40 years later, Wroxham was visited on behalf of the Council for the Preservation of Rural England, by a Dr Cornish, who viewed things a little differently. Having admired the church he turned his attention to the view from Wroxham Bridge, which he dismissed as *'utterly hideous'*. He claimed to be *'dazed by the sight of the haphazard erection of sheds and the indiscriminate lettering of advertisements, even sprawling over the roofs'* Dr Cornish saw it as a prime duty of the planning authority to prevent such excesses. His comments drew a swift riposte from Arnold Roy, the roofs of whose store were one of the 'offenders'. Roy was speaking in his capacity as Chairman of the Wroxham Advancement Association, of which he and John Loynes were important members, unsurprisingly since they were, between them, amongst the principal architects of the rapid commercial growth of the village. More of Roy later.

For a more romantic view of Wroxham, in the 1930s, Arthur Ransome described the village in *Coot Club*:

> *There were boats everywhere, and boats of all kinds, from the big black wherry with her gaily painted mast, loading at the old granary at Wroxham bridge, and meant for nothing but hard work, to the punts of the boatmen going to and fro, and the motor-cruisers filling up with petrol, and the hundreds of big and little yachts tied to the quays, or moored in rows, two or three deep, in the dykes and artificial harbours beside the main river.*

Wroxham in the 1930s.

If Ransome saw *'boats everywhere'* in the 1930s he would surely be at a loss for words were he able to re-visit the bridge today.

The bridge crosses the River Bure and is the umbilical cord which joins

Wroxham Bridge in the 1880s.

Wroxham to the village of Hoveton. It, or its predecessors, have been there a long time; the first stone bridge was built in 1576 to replace an earlier wooden one, and largely rebuilt in 1619.

Much of what visitors take for Wroxham is really Hoveton. The villages, separated just by a narrow stretch of the river, have separate Parish Councils, different District Councils and are in different Parliamentary constituencies. Despite having, just, the larger population, Hoveton's identity has generally become subsumed within the Wroxham 'brand', to the probable frustration of some Hovetonites. Occasionally a skirmish is won, what was Wroxham Railway Station is now Hoveton and Wroxham station, the modern surgery is called the Hoveton and Wroxham Medical Centre, but the whole area is widely known as Wroxham. 'Roys of Wroxham', the self-proclaimed largest village store in the world, is actually in Hoveton but was originally so named because at the time the station was called Wroxham and they sought to avoid confusion with goods and stock delivered by rail. In any event 'Roys of Hoveton' would lack the audible alliterative allure of its current name.

For the avoidance of confusion this booklet will follow the widely accepted convention of referring to the combined parishes as Wroxham. Before I am strung up by irate residents of Hoveton, I would point out that there is a precedent for this—when, in July 1938 preparations started to be put in hand to protect the home front in the event of war, each of the two Parish Councils agreed to amalgamate part of their territory into a single ARP area to be designated as 'Wroxham'.

Wroxham is a place of antiquity. The Domesday Book lists 'Vrocsham' as being held by Stigand, an ecclesiastic who benefited both from family estate holdings in East Anglia and also as a result of intermittent royal patronage, originally from King Cnut but later from Edward the Confessor, who briefly appointed him Bishop of Elmham but deposed him shortly afterwards, before reinstating him just a year later. He was then translated to the Bishopric of Winchester and, while continuing to hold that See, he was appointed Archbishop of Canterbury; an extreme example of the principle of clerical plurality! He acquired huge estates in Norfolk, in Kent, and in Hampshire. He was not a well-thought of man, being seen by many as a manipulative trader in religious privileges. The Domesday Book records that at the time the village comprised 60 acres of land, with two free men, two ploughs and two churches.

Wroxham remained relatively unknown and undeveloped until the arrival of the railway, but both the pre-Domesday period and the interim are worthy of brief mention.

Whether Wroxham was much affected by the Roman occupation is a matter of some dispute; one school promotes the view that there was significant Roman involvement—a ford at the foot of Caen Meadow and possibly a fort at its high point overlooking the river, the other maintains that there is little evidence of any Roman influence at all. Perhaps the most interesting anecdote relates to the reported appearance of an apparition at Wroxham in 1829. A group of gentlemen were sailing on the Broad and decided to moor and enjoy a picnic. Barely had they unloaded the contents of their hampers, they reported, than they were approached by a dishevelled individual whom they assumed was a yokel. Soon they began to feel that he was also a lunatic because he claimed that they were trespassing on land belonging to the Emperor Marcus Aurelius, whose birthday was to be celebrated that day! They pointed out to him that Marcus Aurelius was a man of the 2nd Century, while they were now in the 19th. The figure promptly miraculously transformed into a Roman officer and the party found themselves in a Broad converted to a huge amphitheatre, surrounded by cheering crowds welcoming a procession of soldiers, horses, chariots, lions and followed by hordes of chained prisoners. And they were not the first to report such experiences, more than 100 years earlier a visiting clergyman claimed to have seen something similar. Even earlier, in the early 1600s two young local men, who had gone to the Broad for a swim, had reported that they themselves had been transformed into Roman soldiers to provide a guard for the procession.

Before embarking on an expedition to hunt for such ghosts, the reader may prefer to consider the conclusion of the Broads Authority whose website, when considering the history of Wroxham, states that '*Despite legends of ghostly Roman soldiers seen near the Wroxham Broad, and local rumours of Roman finds–and even a fort–on Caen Meadow, very little evidence for Roman occupation has been found in the area*'.

It is now generally accepted that the Broads were formed as a result of peat digging, predominantly between the 12th and 14th centuries. Digging for peat was a seasonal activity, in the summer. Enough peat would be dug out to provide fuel for the following winter. What is still a source of discussion is the nature of the original diggings. Initially it was assumed that they were large pits, which later filled with water, forming individual Broads as a result of rising sea levels. There is a counter argument that, since peat was dug from boggy areas, such large pits would have flooded anyhow, long before they could have been dug to the depth of the current Broads. The alternative suggestion is still that the Broads were formed from peat pits which had flooded, but that the individual pits were originally much smaller, and the Broads created by the deliberate joining up of these much smaller pits, after they had flooded. Whichever is the case, the conclusion that they were formed from medieval peat diggings rather than being a natural phenomenon does seem to suggest that the Roman amphitheatre in place of the Broad, supposedly seen by the 1829 visitors was a figment of their imagination, as the scene they claimed to have witnessed would have taken place 10 centuries or more before the Broad was formed. Perhaps Norfolk ale was to blame–in the early 19th century there was a scandal involving the use of opium in the brewing process.

In the pre-railway period, the area was largely agricultural, but the reed-beds provided a useful supply for the distinctive Norfolk thatch. Much of the sedge and marsh grass from the river banks was transported by boat to Yarmouth where it was transferred to coasters and taken to London, and used as feed for the horses of the cabs and buses. The arrival of the railway changed everything.

THE ARRIVAL OF THE RAILWAY

The development of the railways arguably had as big an impact on 19th century life as has the computer in the 21st. This is certainly true of life in Wroxham, whose station finally opened in 1874. The railway 'mania' of that period, with lines being proposed regardless of potential viability attracting investment from speculators blindly pursuing the latest thing, was the forerunner of the dotcom boom and bust of more recent times. But setting up a company, issuing a prospectus and even raising the capital were no guarantee that the line proposed would be completed, or even started.

The first proposal for this part of Norfolk had been promulgated nearly 30 years earlier in 1845 as a proposed line from Norwich to Aylsham, with a station in King Street, Norwich, as its base. The proximity of the proposed line to the cathedral may have been in the mind of the satirist who opposed the election of the railway magnate Samuel Morton Peto, as a Norwich MP, by issuing a mock prospectus regretting the necessity of demolishing the Norman masterpiece to make way for a new terminus!

There followed a not untypical series of proposals and counter proposals but it was not until 1860 that plans were submitted to Parliament for a North Walsham line, passing through Wroxham, though no discussion or debate followed for a further three years, when the relevant Acts of Parliament were passed approving the route, but without any reference to the location of stations.

In late 1863 plans were made to incorporate a new company, the East Norfolk Railway (ENR) and build several new lines, amongst them the earlier agreed route to North Walsham from Thorpe, passing through Salhouse and Wroxham, and a further line from Wroxham itself to Horstead, it was intended to be extended to Aylsham when funds allowed. This time the company was incorporated with notables and local landowners such as Lord Suffield and William Trafford as Directors.

Given the earlier delays it is interesting that the relevant Act required completion of the proposed lines within 5 years and it appeared that the East Norfolk Railway had no intention of operating the line themselves, their plan being to contract this out to another company, the Great Eastern–there is little new under the sun!

The plans involved two level crossings in Wroxham, with a station between them located close to the current site of Roys filling station on Norwich Road. Work started but was very slow, and objections were still being raised, notably by

Hoveton and Wroxham station, 2017.

those whose business interests might suffer when the line was complete, such as the wherrymen and the principals of the North Walsham and Dilham Canal company. Discussions continued and changes were made to the original plan, including scrapping the idea of locating the station in residential Wroxham.

A three year extension was granted for the building of the line to North Walsham and a slight change in the routing through Wroxham was also agreed. One result of this was the need to choose a different location for the station and the choice fell upon its present site in Hoveton. The revised date for completion of the line was 30 June 1874, but delays meant that for the line to reach Wroxham a further revised date of somewhere between July and August that year was expected. The good news was that the contractors now held all the land necessary to complete the line right through to North Walsham. Although work was now proceeding well, it didn't prove possible to complete the works in time and it was actually late October by the time the work and the necessary safety surveys had been completed. The line opened on 20 October. Initially the line was to terminate at North Walsham, not by then a sufficiently popular destination to make the line a commercial proposition, and the extension to Cromer, necessary to make the route viable, was delayed while further capital was raised. As with many new routes at the time, insufficient capital had been a problem. One of the reasons for initially planning to build the station in Wroxham had been the shortage of enough capital to build the viaduct to take the line over the river, which, it was feared, might have to be deferred until more capital was raised. Delays were also experienced by the bankruptcy and death of the originally selected contractors and the need to appoint new ones.

By 1877, the route to Cromer was complete, a route to a destination which was already fashionable, in a district which was soon after christened Poppyland by the poet and critic Clement Scott, helping it to become ultra-fashionable. The extended line was patronised by the rich and powerful and Wroxham, a popular stopping point on the route, was a beneficiary. It created an opportunity for commercial growth which was quickly spotted by entrepreneurial locals, of whom two in particular contributed to the development of Wroxham, and whose influence is still very evident more than a century later.

THE BURE VALLEY RAILWAY

The original plan to extend the line to Aylsham was granted in 1876 and a contract was awarded to William Waddell to build the line. It was eventually opened on 1 January 1880. The extension was not a great success with typical passenger numbers being between 5 to 25 on most trains. During the First World War the line was used to carry timber for use as trenching material, but passenger traffic was still light. In 1923 LNER took over the line and traffic increased first with construction of RAF Coltishall, which adjoined the line, and then with the

Bure Valley Railway, No.9 'Mark Timothy' at Wroxham, running onto the turntable, 2014.

onset of World War Two. However, once the war was over, passenger numbers slumped again and British Railways decided to withdraw a passenger service in 1952, eleven years before the infamous Beeching Report. Freight traffic continued but the line was eventually closed on 6 January 1982.

Following the demise of the line, Broadland District Council purchased the section from Wroxham to Aylsham with a view to providing a new footpath, however, railway enthusiasts suggested the construction of a narrow-gauge railway in addition to the footpath along the line of the old route. Construction of the line started on 8 May 1989 and progressed quickly. The line was ready to open with all due ceremony on 10 July 1990 with a locomotive hired from the Romney Hythe and Dymchurch Railway in Kent. Following a turbulent period of ownership, in 2001 the line was acquired by a small group of railway enthusiasts from a business background. Today the Bure Valley Railway carries around 120,000 passengers per year and a heavy train carrying over 200 passengers.

TWO WROXHAM TITANS AND A JOURNALIST

The development of Wroxham in the late 19th century and the first half of the 20th may best be viewed through the lives of two of Wroxham's great characters, responsible for much of the village's growth, both as a holiday destination and as a shopping centre. They each had both vision and flair combined with a serious dose of the work ethic.

John Loynes

One was John Loynes, the man who first came up with the idea of hiring out boats for holiday use, and then went on to develop a fleet on which it was possible for holidaymakers to live and sleep in reasonable comfort. Although his business was later sold, his name lives on in its successor, the hire-boat company, Faircraft Loynes, operating from the Wroxham side of the bridge. Loynes was born on August 24th, 1843 in Woodton, a village close to the border with Suffolk, the son of a boot and shoe repairer. Leaving school at the age of 11 he was put to work to supplement the family income, initially tending sheep and acting as a general labourer. He moved into domestic service near Brooke, where he learnt to sail. Somehow, he managed to save enough to buy himself an apprenticeship as a carpenter. Completing this he joined a firm of master carpenters in Norwich but was ambitious enough to set

John Loynes.

up there in the trade on his own, at Monastery Yard, off Elm Hill. Given his fondness for boating, so the story goes, he bought himself a very old rowing boat in poor condition and dismantled it carefully so he could better understand the principles behind its construction. He then proceeded to build his own small rowing boat, which he hired out for those wanting to row on the Wensum, so successfully that he soon built some more. The story of what happened next is a romantic one, and several versions of it exist. One version is that two young men, Norwich bank clerks, rented a boat for a week and, armed just with a stone jar full of fresh water, a primus stove and an awning under which to sleep, set out for an adventure. Their efforts took them as far as Wroxham, from which, having run out of time, they were unable to return by the lengthy route they had taken. Returning instead by land to Monastery Yard, they explained the situation to John Loynes, who, ever a man of action, set out with a hand cart and a couple of helpers to 'walk' the boat back to Elm Hill. Not long after, two other young men hired his boat and did the same, leaving the boat at Wroxham, 47 miles away by river. Loynes was not keen to repeat his trip with the handcart and decided to hire the boat out from Wroxham, with the landlord of the Kings Head acting as his agent. He was so impressed by the potential of what he saw that he decided to move his operations there. The version published on his 90th birthday in the *Sunday Dispatch* has him pushing the boat in a handcart in the other direction, from Norwich to Wroxham! Other boat-builders, noting his success at Wroxham, imitated him, moving from sites like Coltishall and Beccles.

Whatever the truth of the story, what is beyond doubt is that Loynes did move his business to Wroxham and started trading from there in the 1880s. It is not clear how he raised the capital to expand–it may simply be that he ploughed all his profits back into the business. His ambitions were not simply restricted to Norfolk, either. He began a parallel business in Holland renting out boats to cruise the Friesland Meres. Initially successful, he eventually closed down this branch of his business when

A dyke near Wroxham 1880s.

the unpopularity of the British, especially in Holland, became intense during the Boer Wars.

Although by this time his craft had moved a long way from small open rowing dinghies, development had been gradual. Initially the plan had been to rent out a small boat, with crew, and take the hirer to different locations at which bed and food would be available ashore. But the two young men who had taken the boat to Wroxham must have planted an idea in the mind of John Loynes and he developed awnings which could be slung over the boom to make a crude cover under which to sleep, and from here it was a short step to providing a cabin with a roof which could be lifted when the boat was not under sail to allow sufficient headroom.

John Loynes was a man of remarkable energy. Even at 90 he was still at work, allowing himself a 6-week cruise around the Broads every year as a holiday treat. He remained a great advocate for the Broads, he was President of the Wroxham Advancement Association, chaired by Arnold Roy, and an active campaigner in that Association's long battle with the landowner, T R C Blofeld, to arrange for the reopening of Hoveton Great Broad. He was an inventive imaginative man. When weed threatened the continued viability of Hickling Broad he developed a raft with a machine which could haul up the weed to be transported away from the channel; in his office he developed a model of the Broads, over 20 feet long and incorporating models of his yachts, showing both their rig and their domestic arrangements. This model was transported to exhibitions all over the country to promote his holidays.

At a personal level, we have a picture of him in the article referred to in the

John Loynes, in later life, enjoying a sail and a cup of tea made on the primus. The girl sitting before the mast is the wife of Cecil Chamberlin whose meticulous recording of events there over many years is an indispensable aid to anyone researching Wroxham.

opening paragraph of this book, published in the United States in 1895 when Loynes was in his early 50s. The writer was Anna Bowman Dodd. She describes her arrival in Wroxham and her first sight of Loynes; *'coatless, hatless, lean of shape and sharp of eye'*. Disappointingly, he told her that he had no boat left for hire to her party showing, she wrote, a disappointment *'as keen as our own'*. But Loynes was not a man to disappoint a visitor if he could avoid it. He was kindness itself, explaining the difficulties of high season. He was not the only boat hirer and, suddenly remembering that a rival still had one boat available, he scooped up the transatlantic visitors escorting them to his competitor having sent notice to warn him of the arrival of a potential customer. Yes, the boat was available, Loynes remained with her group for a while to advise them on with what, and where, to provision the boat before they set out. Anna Bowman Dodd was duly grateful, and thoroughly enjoyed her cruise, judging by her article.

In Loynes then we have a man of ambition and imagination, who believed in the virtue of hard work and who treated the customer as special. He was very enterprising, a natural entrepreneur who was willing to take risks, as with his Holland business and another his son went to set up in Canada, and the nous to pull out of enterprises which were not working before they damaged the core business.

And his legacy? By the mid-1920s, Wroxham boasted no less than 11 boatyards, each with its own distinct flag– Loynes chose a White Star and Blue Pennant, while A Collins and Co favoured a white triangle on the almost ubiquitous blue pennant. Only three of the yards chose another colour, two red, and just one yellow. Chamberlin's Guide lists the yards and their telephone numbers, appropriately Loynes had the earliest allocated number, Wroxham 3!

While the efforts of John Loynes and his many imitators brought great economic benefit to the locality, some locals were shocked at the exposure the arrival of visitors brought to modern behaviours and modes. And not just locals, in the summer 1933, The Revd Harold Mullett, from Ponders End, came briefly as a locum clergyman at Hoveton. He was shocked at what he described as the 'nudity' of holiday makers on the Broads and gave an interview to the press, saying *'there is no excuse for nakedness in hot weather, but a desire for the vulgar'* and closed with a few more homilies and references to the Garden of Eden. He created quite a stir, the matter becoming a source of some jocularity at a meeting of the Norwich Rotary Club, when a member strongly took the same view as the Revd Mullett and was rebuffed in humorous style. The subject of the mode of dress also attracted the attention of a visiting journalist from South Africa who wrote in his paper *'some of the most amazing freaks in England seem to find pleasure in boating. Men who look like vegetarians, with beards like dried vermicelli, with shorts and knapsacks take in the delights of Wroxham through horn-rimmed glasses. Women, sometimes abnormally broad in the beam, stuff white silken blouses into the waists of blue serge bell-bottomed trews. They carry walking sticks and smoke cigarettes at the slightest provocation.'*

Such views were probably not front of mind with those whose businesses were benefiting from the growth of visitors, not least the second titan, Arnold Roy.

Arnold Roy

Arnold Roy, one of the founding brothers of Roys of Wroxham, was an exceptionally imaginative retailer whose methods, some of which were imitated by others many years later, enabled him to build a business which was largely based on the Hoveton side of the river. Little more than 30 years after he had opened his first tiny Wroxham store, he was able to make the claim that it was the "World's Largest Village Store". The title is said to have been earned in a competition during the 1930s but no evidence to support this claim remains in the Roys' archive, and Arnold Roy, who delighted in creating slogans, may have devised it. Whether it was one he created, or the result of a genuine competition, may be open to debate but the size of his business, even then, was not.This was widely recognised, not just in Britain–in 1935 an article in the *Johannesburg Sunday Times* described the store as being *'as big as any three of the largest general stores in Johannesburg put together'*.

Arnold Roy was the son of the village carpenter in Reepham. Roy (senior) also ran the village store there, so retailing was in the blood of Arnold and his brother Alfred, who co-founded the store with him. Alfred was the more conventional brother, with his feet firmly on the ground. Arnold was the more mercurial, and an entrepreneur from an early age. As a child he was given a mule, made a cart and, stocking it from his father's village store, trudged round the neighbouring hamlets selling his goods. Both brothers went briefly to London, where Arnold made a special point of observing the methods and practices of the big stores–he soon convinced himself that anything they could do, he could do as well, or better.

Arnold Roy.

Returning to Norfolk he spotted an opportunity to buy a shop in Coltishall, at the time a thriving village dependant largely on its malting industry. He approached his father for a loan to buy the shop, who agreed on the understanding that the business was run by both brothers, and one of their sisters, Katie. It wasn't long before Katie married and moved to Fakenham, where she and her husband opened a shop of their own.

Coltishall was already a thriving place with a much larger population than Wroxham, approaching 2000 at the time, and as well as the maltings had a successful boat building industry, but Arnold's eye was on what was happening at Wroxham. There the railway had led to the rapid development of the hire boat business. In those early days, hirers were arriving not by car with stocks of food and other necessities in the boot, but by train, and their need to buy provisions was clear to Arnold Roy. Leaving his brother to carry on running the successful Coltishall store, he opened the first Wroxham store in 1899. It was tiny, but as was Arnold's way the store claimed to be 'Universal Providers'. His gift for self-advertisement was so great that just about the only thing he didn't stock was a bushel under which to hide his own light. Originally, he appointed a Mr Carver to manage the new store but he was so anxious to develop the store along the lines he envisaged that soon he had himself replaced Mr Carver, despite a petition from the existing customers. Arnold Roy targeted the boat hire audience and for over 60 years Roys' catalogues, eventually running to over 150 pages, were sent out by the boatyards to those booking holidays, offering just about everything the hirer could want for delivery to the boat. The Hoveton born poet and author, Alan

Hunter, later to become best known for his Inspector Gently mysteries, had, as a young man, published a collection of poems one of which, *Saturday at Wroxham* (Saturday at that time being the normal start day for boat hire) having directed the reader to 'Roys Corner', in a few lines summed up the universality of what was available there:

The first Wroxham store, 1899.

> I want provision for a cruise
> I want some tins of Heinzes' stews!
> I want bacon and some bread –
> No–I'll take crispbread instead.
> Where do I get paraffin?
> Cut the ham up nice and thin!
> Can I buy fishing tackle here?
>
> Stop me buy one, two or three,
> Strawberry for you, Vanilla for me!
> Let's buy sun-glasses and a map,
> A guide book and a yachting cap,
> Sun-burn lotion, films and camera
> What glorious impedimenta!

But Arnold Roy would not have been satisfied with just the hire boat trade– even though it was said that at one time his relationship with the Wroxham hire companies was so strong that every item on every boat, from mattress to cooking utensil had been supplied by him. He built a huge local clientele, and his methods were a long way ahead of his time. For the boat hirers he came up with a deal whereby any unused tinned food would be bought back by Roys at the end of the holiday at full price and, in addition to supplies, he also rented out gramophones with a selection of records; devotees of Arthur Ransome's *Coot Club* will immediately think of the Hullabaloos.

For locals he came up with a range of ideas. He provided cars and drivers to bring important customers into the store, and with new lines he engaged in outbound telemarketing before the term was invented. But he was happy to use traditional methods too. One of the businesses in the Roys stable was a bakery and the roundsmen were an integral part both of this business and of the general store. Roundsmen always had at least one item they were able to sell at or below cost price. This loss leader helped to establish Roys as a good value retailer.

One of Arnold Roy's favourite slogans was 'a wireless set for every cottage' and he developed a range of original marketing plans to promote their sale. One particularly striking example was the weekend use of his store as a dance venue. Part of the shop floor was cleared and dances were held to music broadcast on the wireless. Some of these were decorous affairs, but on occasion he would hold a pyjama dance, with special buses laid on from Norwich and Great Yarmouth at which flappers could dance the Charleston and the Black Bottom where their mothers had been shopping earlier in the day. And he didn't stop at dances–he held concerts too, again using broadcast music, on Sunday evenings, but to make sure he didn't offend anyone, these were always timed to start after Evensong had finished. Another of his plans was to combine public service with the promotion of the sale of wireless sets by hosting other events. During the General Election in 1924 the *Eastern Daily Press* reported '*Mr Arnold Roy's wireless programme at Wroxham last week attracted between 300 and 400 listeners to the speeches of Mr Ramsay MacDonald, Mr Baldwin and Mr Asquith. For Wroxham it was a unique election experience.*' Baldwin was, nationally, the winner, overturning the Labour/Liberal coalition which had been the result of an election the previous year with a landslide victory which returned the Conservatives with a majority of more than 200. The *Eastern Daily Press* report ended by identifying the type of set, the type of aerial and the type of speakers used. Arnold Roy rarely missed an opportunity to promote a product he stocked.

But he was much more than just an exceptional retailer. His was the face of Wroxham–he was the subject of numerous articles in both the trade and

The crossroads known as 'Roys corner' showing today's store and food hall on the right which also houses a McDonalds restaurant, 2020.

national press—one paper christened him the Norfolk Napoleon, a slightly ironic nickname given Napoleon's alleged sneering dismissal of the English as 'a nation of shopkeepers'. He appeared on the wireless himself—it was on the popular programme *In Town Tonight* that he developed his assertion of being a 'universal provider' by saying that at Roys a customer could acquire '*anything from a pin to an elephant*'.

He took a leading role in the public life of Wroxham, as the long-term Chairman of the Wroxham Advancement Association, as a local councillor and as a Justice of the Peace. He was a generous supporter of the village, providing its street lights and its public lavatory. Wroxham had, and has, a great deal for which to be grateful to Arnold Roy.

But it was not all work—the *Eastern Daily Press* reporting that while playing golf at Mundesley on the 8 July 1932 he had achieved a hole in one at the 166 yard 6th hole. For the public announcement of this achievement he was indebted to the paper's local agent.

Cecil Chamberlin

Much of what we know about Wroxham in the 1920s and 1930s we know thanks to Cecil Chamberlin. He kept a shop on the bridge, primarily a news agency but with many other lines. He was a notable voluntary public servant, with a finger in just about every village activity and group. Having originally worked as an assistant to Arnold Roy, retail was clearly no mystery to him, but his greatest pleasure came from his role as the local correspondent of the *Eastern Daily Press* which he remained for over 30 years. Carefully he pasted into his book all his contributions both to the EDP and the occasional piece in the

Cecil Chamberlin shop.

national press. Copies of most of them are now available at Wroxham Library in a couple of thick files, and they present a very intimate picture not just of the development of the Broads but most interestingly of what was happening socially at the time, with reports from all sorts of local groups and clubs from dramatic societies to the Good Companions Club. His original scrapbooks, loaned to me by his daughter, Rita Massingham, contain an added bonus because not only did he keep a meticulous record of what he had been paid for each contribution but he also retained other correspondence. On one occasion the EDP questioned his expense account, his response was so comprehensive that in the end they admitted he was right. My favourite is a letter from the *Sunday Dispatch* in 1933 instructing him to telephone immediately should a big story occur at any time on Saturday night or on Sunday… *'it is essential that not a second shall be lost'*, and promising *'special rates for big news scoops on a Sunday—every second counts'*.

One of Chamberlin's most important roles was as Secretary of the Wroxham Advancement Association, chaired by Arnold Roy and with John Loynes as President, so he knew both titans well. They must have made a formidable trio.

THREE CHURCHES AND TWO HOUSES

Wroxham and Hoveton churches

Of the two churches listed in the Domesday Book, the location of St Mary's remains as in medieval times, as the Parish Church of Wroxham. Hoveton has two churches, St John and St Peter. Each is noteworthy in its own way.

St Mary's was effectively at the centre of the medieval settlement. The current church, largely of flint, dates mainly back to the 15th century, although some stonework is from the 12th century. Pevsner was particularly taken with the south doorway, of Norman origin. He described the doorway as *'barbaric and glorious'*! Its columns are of special interest being ornately carved. The oak door itself dates from the 15th century.

Hoveton can boast two fine churches, St John's and St Peter's. St John's, a church of 11th century origins was subject to the not unusual Victorian 'improvement'.

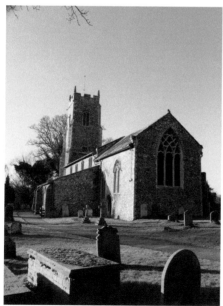

St Mary's, Wroxham, 2020.   *Norman south doorway, 2020.*

Detail on the columns of the south doorway of St Mary's, Wroxham, 2020.

There are several interesting features. The brick tower was built in the late 19th century, replacing a medieval one which had been destroyed by a lightning strike, and the sixteenth century scissor roof, which was only re-discovered in the 1950s.

St Peter's is a small but beautiful thatched church, dating from the early 17th century, again restored in the late Victorian era.

Each of the three churches is still used as a place of worship, and all are a pleasure to visit.

St Peter's, Hoveton, 2020.

A TALE OF TWO HOUSES

For many years Wroxham had two major houses, Wroxham Hall, and Wroxham House. Both have been demolished, Wroxham House in the 1950s, Wroxham Hall in about 1960. The Hall was purchased by the Trafford family in the early 19th century from the Collyers, and the estate remains in Trafford hands to this day. Amongst the property the estate still hold is Wroxham Broad

Wroxham Hall.

itself. Wroxham House was the property of Colonel S F Charles, after whom Charles Close off the Avenue is named, its houses being constructed on what was at one time a part of his estate.

The Traffords, a Catholic family, whose family mausoleum stands proud in the churchyard of the Anglican St Mary's Church, had their own family chapel and chaplain. The mausoleum was erected by Margaret, the widow of Sigismund Trafford, who had fought at the battle of Waterloo. The architect employed in 1827 to design the mausoleum was Anthony Salvin, many of whose commissions were in respect of country houses but who also worked locally on the re-facing of

The Trafford family mausoleum, 2020.

Norwich Castle and the re-modelling of the West Front of Norwich Cathedral. The mausoleum, now sealed, is a very striking building and one strange to find in an Anglican churchyard.

In 1885 the Traffords acquired the Broad itself, and enthusiastically encouraged the development of competitive sailing. E S Trafford was in 1860 Commodore of the then Norfolk and Suffolk Yacht Club, having been Vice Commodore in its foundation year of 1859. But the relationship between the Traffords and the village was not always sweetness and light. Around the beginning of the 20th century there was a case involving a right of way between Wroxham and the neighbouring village of Crostwick. The path, a favourite Sunday ramble for locals for many years, abutted Trafford land and in parts encroached upon it. The squire at the time decided to put a stop to these incursions which he felt could damage his property and potentially scare his game birds. His response, apparently without consultation or warning, was to erect a series of gates, and the following Sunday these were manned by his gamekeepers, who turned away the villagers seeking to use the footpath. He had failed to take into account that acts of 'enclosure' have always been resisted in Norfolk—the spirit of Kett lives on! The local villagers decided to resist, though they didn't arm themselves with weapons as in Kett's time, but with the law—they took the case to court, and won. In an age when deference, especially in the country, was still the norm, feelings must have run very high for the villagers to confront their squire this way. Reputedly the squire took the result badly and virtually ignored the village from then on. It has been suggested that, as a result of giving evidence in the case some estate workers lost their jobs, but I have found no corroboration of this. Today, matters are different—it seems quite an irony that the Trafford Estate offered, in 2019, to provide a new footpath for the village along part of the Avenue.

If the village relationship with the Traffords has had its ups and downs, the same could not be said for their neighbours at Wroxham House, Colonel and Mrs Charles. Colonel Charles was a veteran of the Boer War and a friend of Baden-Powell, who apparently used to visit Wroxham to see his old friend and enjoy a sail on the Broad.

Colonel Charles was an enthusiastic supporter of the Scout Movement, and encouraged the establishment of a troop in Wroxham as early as 1910, the year in which Baden-Powell retired from the army and founded the Boy Scouts Association, though his original camp at Brownsea Island had been held three years earlier. When Baden-Powell visited Wroxham in 1914 he personally presented a flag to the Wroxham troop. As the movement grew, Colonel Charles became County Commissioner and took a particularly keen interest in the local troop. In *Four Poplars*, the delightfully nostalgic story of his Wroxham childhood, the Rev Clifford Davies relates the many kindnesses shown by Colonel and Mrs Charles to the local scouts. They were welcome to use the many acres that surrounded the house, giving them access to Broad frontage. They were provided with a shed on the estate to use as a Headquarters and the Colonel always visited the shed on Scout evenings and also visited the annual camp on the coast where he would award prizes for various activities. As well as the annual camp there would be weekends spent camping on the Wroxham House estate. In less clement weather the boys would be invited to the Colonel's study with its great log fire, where he would read to them, and lead a discussion on Baden-Powell's ideas, the evening finishing with a hymn accompanied by Mrs Charles on the piano, and the consumption of some special treats from the kitchen.

Colonel and Mrs Charles may not have been of local origin, but they clearly felt an obligation to the community, one which they seem to have discharged with both charm and enthusiasm.

WROXHAM IN WORLD WAR TWO

Wroxham's by then dominant industry of building and hiring out holiday craft came to a standstill, as there were limits on pleasure boating. Between 1941 and mid 1942 it was banned altogether but Wroxham benefited when the restrictions were slightly lifted as it was privately-owned, allowing yacht racing to take place on the Broad. There was concern that the Broads might be used by enemy floatplanes as part of an invasion and many hire boats and some wherries were deliberately anchored in both Wroxham and Hickling Broads as a deterrent; some launches were armed as patrol boats.

The boatyards were rapidly adapted to replace the building of holiday craft with those for the use of the Admiralty and the RAF. The range of craft they built was substantial; the workers were exempt from conscription, but had to be supplemented by additional workers, some of whom were accommodated in those boats from the hire fleets which were not being used as obstacles to the landing of floatplanes.

In Wroxham one of the yards which converted for war work was that of Graham Bunn (later re-named Windboats). Typical of the boats they built was HDML 1308, a 72 foot Harbour Defence Launch, completed in 1943. This class of boat was used for a wide range of service, from acting as a spotter for enemy submarines to marking the mine-free channels

HDML 1308, built in Wroxham.

for the D Day landings. The boats were built of wood, predominantly teak and mahogany, and were deployed in many theatres of war, boats for the tropics having a copper sheath added to the wooden hull. Boats were originally transferred to distant locations as deck cargo on merchant ships, but later went out under their own power. There was even a plan at one time to rig them with temporary masts to enable them to reach their station under sail.

While the building of naval vessels was an obvious way for Wroxham to help in the war effort, the village made another, more secret, contribution. Even before the war began planning was under way nationally to organise local resistance in the event of invasion. By 1940, with the enthusiastic support of Churchill, a range of 'Operational Bases' had been built in key areas. These were underground chambers, each offering a base for a small group of specially trained auxiliary forces. These men were selected in part for their local knowledge and a perceived ability to live rough. Their role, in the event of invasion, was to impede in every way possible the progress of any invading force and to liaise with the conventional armed forces by the provision of information on enemy dispositions and strengths. The role was very dangerous, it was assumed that the life expectancy of the men, after invasion, would be very short, and those selected were required to sign the Official Secrets Act before being given any detail of their task.

Wroxham was certainly the site of at least one of these operational bases, though not one of the early ones, and possibly of two. The known underground base was situated just off The Avenue, in the grounds of Beech House. Such bases were intended to accommodate a team of 6 or 7 men on a full- time basis if it became necessary. They were equipped with an assortment of weaponry and a range of explosive material, which the men learnt to disguise. The plan was that they should lie low in the day, emerging at night to seek out and destroy enemy assets. They were also trained in unarmed combat and the use of German weaponry in case they captured any. In the event, of course, the invasion didn't happen and the only explosive incident involving the Wroxham base occurred when a team member accidentally ignited a bottle of gas, injuring one of his colleagues. The Officer Commanding all Norfolk Auxiliary Units promptly issued an instruction telling his men to check Calor Gas bottles were switched off before lighting a match! As invasion fears receded some of the men were re-deployed. Two from the Wroxham unit were recruited into the SAS where they operated behind enemy lines in occupied France after the Normandy landings. Sadly both, with most of their team, were betrayed and their camp attacked. Breaking out they with about 30 others were captured and, having been made to dig out a communal grave, were executed summarily under Hitler's specific requirement that commandos should be executed, not imprisoned.

THE POST WAR SITUATION

The ending of the war did not mean that Wroxham could immediately return to its traditional industry. Some of the boats moored in the Broad to deter enemy seaplanes had sunk, others were in very poor condition and some of these were only useful for demolition to provide wood and parts to help restore others; make do and mend was the order of the day. Even where a usable fleet of hire boats was available, the shortage of fuel meant that hirers were restricted to a very limited cruising range. In 1947 the basic petrol ration stopped altogether and the following year a means of identifying petrol intended for commercial use was brought in with an additive of red dye. The writer can, just, remember random checks being carried out by police stopping private cars and testing the contents of the fuel tank for red dye. The cartoonist Osbert Lancaster's take on the situation was a cartoon in which the glamorous lady passenger of a driver found using commercial petrol is shown explaining to the policeman that she had inadvertently dropped her nail varnish into the petrol tank! The penalties for breaking the rules were high–the driver was banned from driving for a year, and any garage caught selling commercial fuel for private use could be closed down. In the same year a more limited basic ration was introduced. It wasn't until 1950 that petrol finally came off the ration, and the hire business could resume its pre-war trend of growth.

The lack of available material limited the amount of boat building which could be done, but it was in this period that Wroxham metaphorically dipped its toe briefly in the car industry. The North Walsham Heritage Centre provides, on its website, perhaps the most comprehensive explanation of the work of Duncan Industries, a company established by Ian Duncan, a mechanical engineer with an

Wooden frames for Duncan cars.

The Healey Duncan, Paris Motor Show 1947.

aeronautical background to build cars, or at least the aluminium bodies of cars. They were to be built on wooden frames, using ash. Some of these frames had as many as 62 pieces, fixed together with the type of glue which had been used in the manufacture of Mosquito aircraft during the war. The range of skills needed to produce such frames was similar to that involved in boat-building and it was a natural step for Duncan to involve a number of yards in the project.

Sadly it proved only a short term boost to the local economy. Although Duncan developed relationships with a number of top manufacturers, Alvis and Healey amongst them, only about 60 or 70 cars for those two brands were built before, after just 2 years, the company went into liquidation. The Healey Duncan was an exceptionally stylish car, and with a top speed of over 100 mph it was the fastest production sports car in the world when it was shown at the Paris Motor Show in 1947.

A stylish Alvis Duncan.

For Wroxham's major retailer the early post war years were not comfortable either. The founding brothers of Roys were getting older and their grip on the detail of the business had diminished. Alfred had, shortly before the war, suggested that the company had grown to a size where professional and managerial specialist staff would be of benefit, but Arnold, always the big picture man, disagreed, and nothing was done. By the end of the war the cracks were more evident, certainly to Fred Roy, Alfred's son, who returning from the war came into the firm in 1946, and quickly recognised the need to tighten things up if the store was to retain its profitability. To make the changes necessary to keep the business viable, he set out moving from the Coltishall store to the Wroxham one, with less than total cooperation from some longer serving staff.

In the early 1950s both founding brothers died, first Alfred in 1951 and then, in 1953, Arnold. This meant that large Estate Duty bills had to be paid, and the situation was worse because Arnold, who had never married, had left his shares outside the family, to a long-serving employee. Alfred had left his estate to his children though most of it was tied up in the business and the funds to pay the duty were only raised with some difficulty. With the death of Arnold more funds had to be raised, both for duty and to pay off Arnold's heir, who wanted to sell his shares. Properties were sold, others mortgaged and a firm of management consultants were brought in to advise. Their advice was unequivocal–sell the business. The family resisted, and in Fred Roy had the champion they needed. Having cleared the decks by filling in and then plastering over the cracks in the business processes and by raising the wind to buy the non-family held shares, he set out to re-build the business, applying lessons he had learned while travelling in Australia and then the United States. A key to his philosophy was that to succeed a retailer had to make his business car-friendly and he achieved just that. Even today Roys must be one of the easiest places for a motorist to shop, with the store virtually surrounded by free car parks. It may sound simple but it was actually a very complex task involving major changes in the road layout of the village. Fred Roy's turn-round of the business was so widely recognised that in 1972 the *Sunday Times* ran a double page spread lauding his achievements. Given his determination to make life easy for the motorist it is appropriate enough that the article began '*In Norfolk, all roads lead to Roys*'.

But not everything was black in those early post-war years. There were some who could see huge potential for the boat business and were prepared to invest in its future. Donald Hagenbach, a Yorkshire businessman with a fondness for Broadland, was browsing through *The Times* while travelling by train between Leeds and London in 1946. His eye was drawn to an advertisement for the sale of a Norfolk boatyard. Almost on a whim he and his wife travelled down to Wroxham that weekend, looked over the yard, liked it, made an offer to Graham Bunn, the owner, negotiated a reduction in the deposit to 5%, which he could manage only by arranging an overdraft and bought it. He was to own the yard for nearly 30 years, re-naming the business Windboats and making a huge success of it. He sold the business only when he retired in 1974 and it is still thriving today, though now in nearby North Walsham rather than Wroxham.

I am indebted to Donald Hagenbach's daughter, Penny Keens, for the story of how her father came to buy the yard, and also for a delightful anecdote which reminds us of the continued USAF presence in those post-war years. Before moving to Wroxham, Hagenbach had bought a plot of land in Horning. When an opportunity arose in Wakefield to buy a large wooden shed which had been in use as a small factory, for £25, he snapped it up, and transported it to Norfolk. To get to his plot it was necessary to make the final stage by water, and with one helper, he loaded the shed on to, a lighter, slightly smaller than the shed itself, and they gingerly 'rowed' it down to the site where it was re-erected and improved by the addition of a small kitchen. The Hagenbachs intended to come down from Wakefield to use it as a holiday home. When they were not there the property was 'looked after' by a local acquaintance. One day Donald Hagenbach was contacted by the West Yorkshire police and asked if he were acquainted with the individual concerned. When he had explained the connection the police suggested that Donald Hagenbach should go down to the property as soon as possible. He found out why only on his arrival when he discovered that the trusted acquaintance had decided to make a profit out of his stewardship by turning the house into a brothel for the use of USAF personnel. Hagenbach recorded that this discovery was enough to make his wife decide that they would never stay there again!

And it wasn't just businessmen who were attracted to post-war Wroxham. One famous new resident was a customer of Windboats, two of whose cruisers he owned, the second being built by them for him. Both boats were named after his wife, Beryl. The new resident was George Formby who had first visited the Broads in the 1940s and later purchased a house in Wroxham. Formby was believed by many to be thoroughly under Beryl's thumb, but she was certainly an effective manager. At

George Formby at Roys.

one time, in the 1950s he was earning £1500 per week–about £40,000 in today's value. Formby became a part of Wroxham life, even opening a department for Roys (right). The photograph shows Formby and the formidable Beryl with Fred Roy on the right. As Formby was reputed to be nearly illiterate it is interesting that he appears to be reading his speech. Given that Wroxham's street lighting had originally been a gift from Arnold Roy one might have expected Roys to have constructed an imitation one for him to lean against while performing the ceremony!

After the war Arnold Roy and Cecil Chamberlin were still prominent in local life, and both featured in a BBC broadcast of the programme *Country Magazine*

in 1947. Arnold Roy is the third from
the left, Cecil Chamberlin the second
from the right. Others in the picture
are Sidney Grapes, author of the much
loved 'Boy John' letters written in dialect
and published in the *Eastern Daily Press*,
still a delight to read 60 years after the
death of their author, local farmers
Jack Borrett and John Howes, and Jack
Powles–another Wroxham boat-building

Titan, Ralph Wightman (BBC) and
Phyllis Painter, landlady of the King's

BBC recording of Country Magazine.

Head, from whose premises the programme was broadcast.

THE BROAD AND THE VILLAGE TODAY

The Broads in general, and arguably Wroxham Broad in particular, have

The lateener Maria.

become a paradise for the leisure sailor.
From the early 19th century there were
'water frolics'–generally friendly and
entertaining contests between mainly
working boats–the Broads and their
rivers were still an important conduit
of trade. But it wasn't long before the
competitive instincts of the leisured
classes demanded boats designed for
racing, and new designs quickly followed.
One early type of boat was the lateener,
an example of which, the *Maria*, built in

1827, is still to be seen in the Museum of the Broads.

The popularity of sailing grew rapidly and soon the leisured classes were joined

by the professional middle classes and
new designs abounded. Water frolics
became Regattas. As the competitive
nature of the racing grew, Wroxham
became a particular favourite, its large
expanse, over 80 acres, and the lack
of natural obstructions such as islands
made it especially suitable as a venue
for racing. Today Wroxham is the home
of the Norfolk Broads Yacht Club, as
it has been since 1937, formed by an

An Edwardian view of Wroxham Broad.

amalgamation of a number of other clubs when an opportunity arose to lease the Broad. Its Wroxham Week is perhaps the most spectacular event of its kind on the Broads.

The Broads today are enjoyed both by the sailing enthusiast and the motor-cruiser driving holiday maker, most of whom, even if they hire elsewhere, spend at least a short while in Wroxham. They are supplemented by huge numbers of day visitors who enjoy the regular short Broads trips. And the river is not the only attraction, the railway enthusiast is well catered for too. The Barton House Railway, a miniature riverside railway and its accompanying museum and buildings, is a delight to children and their parents and, when the weather is poor, there is always Wroxham Miniature Worlds to visit, with its remarkable range of railway layouts from around the world.

ACKNOWLEDGMENTS

I would like to express my appreciation of the help and support given by a number of those to whom Wroxham, and its history, are particularly dear. Those who have been especially generous with their time and their knowledge include Peter Bower, Spencer Brooke, Keith Turner, Rita Massingham, Penny Keens, Richard Riley, Peter Pank and Trevor Curson.

I would also like to thank Paul Roy for allowing me to use again material and illustrations arising from my research in the Roys archive for a previous book. Bob Wright of the North Walsham Heritage Group and Wayne Beauchamp of the North Walsham Archive each took great trouble in tracking down information on Duncan Industries and I am grateful to them both.

I would also like to draw attention to two websites, not specifically about Wroxham but full of detail on which to draw. That of The Medusa Trust whose encyclopaedic records enabled me to discover more about the wartime work of the boatyards and that of The British Resistance Archive which relates the story of the underground bunker at Beech House.

SOME FURTHER READING:

Armstrong, C.	*Anything From a Pin to an Elephant: Tales of Norfolk Retail*, 2016
Goodrum, P.	*Norfolk Broads: The Biography*, 2014
Mitchell, L.	*Slow Travel: Norfolk*, 2018
Ransome, A.	*The Coot Club: A Norfolk Broads Adventure*, 1934
Rouse, M.	*Norfolk Through Time*, 2014

Index